THE WORLD OF THE

COYOTE

ACKNOWLEDGEMENTS

Among the many people who have helped me during the research and writing of this book, I particularly want to thank Mike Gibeau, Colleen Campbell and Paul Paquet, who are conducting valuable wild canine studies in Banff National Park, Alberta. I also want to thank Bob Crabtree, of Bozeman, Montana, for taking time out of a harried week to patiently answer my questions, and Kezha Hatier, for letting me tag along with her in Yellowstone National Park, Wyoming. In addition, Mike Gibeau and Bob Crabtree reviewed the first draft of this book and made many helpful suggestions. Others who have helped greatly include Arlen Todd, Dennis Voigt, Mike Buss, Maria Delmeida, Dean Cluff and Arnold Boer.

I am also grateful to Candace Savage for her wise counsel and warm hospitality during the book's formative stages. To Nancy Flight, whose editorial advice has been much appreciated and often followed. To Reg Martin, Pam Green, Kenneth de Kok and Carolyn Smart for their friendship and support. And, throughout this project as for so many others, to Merilyn Simonds Mohr, the reader over my shoulder.

FACING PAGE: RICK McINTYRE

I N T R O D U C T I O N

I'm the voice of all the Wildest West, the Patti of the Plains;
I'm a wild Wagnerian opera of diabolic strains;
I'm a roaring, ranting orchestra with lunatics becrammed;
I'm a vocalized tornado—I'm the shrieking of the damned.

—Ernest Thompson Seton, "The Coyote's Song," 1913

The first time I heard coyotes howling was on a cold, clear night in late October in eastern Ontario. I had just stepped outside to look up at the stars when I heard a sudden ghostlike chorus of rising and falling ululations coming from the other side of a granite ridge that cuts across a muskrat swamp to the south of the cabin. I listened for nearly half an hour, caught by the haunting melody, fascinated by what was obviously not just a random series of howls but parts of a conversation. The sounds seemed to tremble on the verge of language, to be, almost literally, the voice of the wilderness.

I have since learned that coyotes howl for a number of reasons, most of which are understood only by coyotes. "They are the most vocal of all North American wild mammals," writes H. T. Gier, a wildlife biologist at the University of Kansas, "but unfortunately, coyote communications have not been analyzed." Like wolves and birds, members of a coyote pack vocalize to keep in touch with one another, as well as for other reasons. The scientific name for the coyote, *Canis latrans*, means "barking dog," and the epithet is well deserved: wolves rarely bark, and foxes rarely talk outside of mating season, but a short, sharp yip from a

FACING PAGE: *A coyote pounces on its tiny prey. Coyotes differ from wolves in that they hunt alone and up to 80 per cent of their diet consists of rodents.* JEFF FOOTT

PART 1

COYOTES & NATURE

Coyotes often seek out high vantage points from which to scout out the surrounding territory. ESTHER SCHMIDT/VALAN PHOTOS

COYOTES & NATURE

Gliding about in their shady forest homes, keeping
well out of sight, there is a multitude of sleek
clad animals living and enjoying their clean,
beautiful lives. How beautiful and interesting they are
is about as difficult for busy mortals to find out
as if their homes were beyond sight in the sky.

—John Muir, "The Forests of Oregon," 1880

FIRST ENCOUNTERS

On a warm afternoon in late July, as I was driving along a narrow, winding road in Banff National Park, Alberta, I interrupted the progress of a mother coyote and three pups as they were crossing from a steep, pine-covered slope on the right to a low meadow on the left. The female and two of the pups had made it safely across, but my approach had stranded the third pup halfway up the slope on the right. When I pulled over to the side of the road, I could see him through the lodgepole pines, wanting to continue, hesitating, starting forward again, then backing up. He reminded me of an over-eager base runner waiting for the sign to steal second.

Down among the wolf willows, Mama simply sat down with her two young ones to wait for me to leave. As she waited, the two pups gamboled beside her, rolling over each other, chewing at each other's ears, attacking blades of grass and otherwise behaving like a pair of

FACING PAGE: *A female coyote*
plays with her month-old pups.
Pups are born in early May, leave
the den in June and remain with
their mother until the fall.
W. PERRY CONWAY

A coyote pack consists of a dominant, or alpha, pair and one or more associate family members, depending on the availability of food. TOM & PAT LEESON

THE PACK

A coyote pack consists of three to eight animals, with an average of around six. The nucleus of the pack is the mating pair, also known as the alpha pair; these are the two dominant animals of the pack. There are also two or more associate or beta coyotes, younger adults whose main role is to defend the pack's territory and to help look after the pups and the nursing mother. Under normal pack situations, only the alpha pair breeds, so only the alpha female bears pups. Beta females do not even mate unless the coyote population is severely threatened, in which case the beta female will sometimes bear pups in the same den and at the same time as the alpha female. This phenomenon, however, is rare in natural

A pack's home range is around 15 square kilometres (5.8 square miles), slightly larger in winter.
TOM & PAT LEESON

Sometimes coyotes howl for the sheer joy of self-expression—in the words of one researcher, giving voice to "some deeper feelings and needs of the caller."

DON ZIPPERT

THE OUTBREAK OF HOSTILITIES

It is hard to pinpoint exactly when the first shot was fired in the war against the coyote. The Spanish seem to have taken a dislike to the animal almost at first sight. The earliest European account of the coyote is found in a Latin text, *Nova Plantarum, Animalium et Mineralium Mexicanorum Historia,* published by Francisco Hernández in 1651. Hernández describes the *coyotl* as having "a wolf-like head, lively large pale eyes, small sharp ears, a long, dark, and not very thick muzzle, sinewy legs with thick crooked nails, and a very thick tail. Its bite is harmful." He then leaves natural history behind to delve into hearsay:

> It is said to attack and kill not only sheep and similar animals but also stags and sometimes even men. . . . It is a persevering revenger of injuries and, remembering prey once snatched from it, if it recognizes the thief days afterward it will give chase. Sometimes it will even attack a pack of its own breed and if possible bite and kill them.

A later reference, in the *History of Mexico,* written in 1780 by Francisco Javier Clavijero, is less damaging to the coyote's image: "*Coyotl,*" wrote Clavijero, "is one of the most common quadrupeds of Mexico, in form like the dog, voracious like the lobo, astute like the fox, in some qualities resembling the jackal."

When Lewis and Clark made their foray to the West in 1804, they travelled almost to the foothills of the Rockies before encountering coyotes, or "burrowing dogs," as they called this new (to them) animal. Merriwether Lewis, in his journal entry for 5 May 1805, also called it "the small wolf," and noted that it was

> of intermediate size between the fox and dog, very delicately formed, fleet and active. The ears are large, erect and pointed; the head is long and pointed, like that of the fox; the tail long and bushy; the hair and fur are of a pale reddish-brown color, though much coarser than that of the fox; the eye is of a deep sea-green color, small and piercing; the talons are rather longer than those of the wolf of the Atlantic States, which animal, as far as we can perceive, is not to be found on this side of the Platte. These wolves usually associate in bands of ten or twelve, and are rarely if ever seen alone, not being able singly to attack a deer or antelope. They live and rear their young in burrows, which they fix near some pass or spot much frequented by game, and sally out in a body against any animal which they think they can overpower; but on the slighest alarm retreat to their burrows making a noise exactly like that of a small dog.

The war entered its official phase towards the middle of the nineteenth century, when ranchers began raising livestock on the American and Canadian prairies; coyote eradication

years—PARC was renamed Wildlife Services in the 1960s, then Animal Damage Control (ADC), and has now gone back to Wildlife Services—the war against the coyote is far from over. In 1992 alone, ADC "biological science technicians" killed 97,966 coyotes, nearly twice as many as all other "nuisance animals" combined, except songbirds.

Once the voice of the untamed American desert, the coyote is now one of the most persecuted of predators. RICK McINTYRE

Leg-hold traps and poisons have been used to exterminate the coyote from farm and range land.

MICHAEL H. FRANCIS

HOW TO KILL A COYOTE

The "how" of coyote control is a compendium of increasingly effective and inhumane methods. The early government hunters, known as *los coyoteros* in Mexico, or simply as federal coyote men farther north, used rifles and steel leg-hold traps—simple devices that snap two metal jaws together when an animal steps on a trip-release mechanism between the jaws. Although the unpadded leg-hold has come under fire in recent years as an inhumane method of trapping any animal, for most of this century it has been the main weapon in the hunter's arsenal. A study conducted in Alberta in 1990 found that injuries to coyotes caught in unpadded leg-hold traps ranged from small lacerations and muscle damage to compound fractures, separation of elbow and hock joints, freezing and gangrene, and actual limb amputation—the last occurring in two of the eighty-two coyotes included in the study. One coyote, the report states drily, "caught at the mid-carpal area, escaped with the trap on its foot. It was sighted 12 days later with the trap still attached. At this time, the coyote appeared to be thin and moved slowly. After another 10 days, it was seen with the trap and the trapped foot missing."

Later hunters, like Charles Cadieux, author of *Coyotes: Predators and Survivors*, who worked for the ADC in the 1960s, shot coyotes from airplanes and helicopters, which were owned by sheep ranchers and operated by the Department of the Interior. Or else they tracked the coyotes to their dens and fished out their pups with hooked wires: "After an hour of hard digging," Cadieux writes, "we were able to cable out seven pups by using a piece of telephone guy-wire with the ends unraveled and bent back to form hooks. An expert with this tool could tangle it in the hide of any coyote and pull him, protesting, to his fate." Cadieux also writes about tossing cyanide gas canisters into dens, igniting them and then covering up the den openings, causing the pups to die "quickly and almost painlessly." Less meticulous hunters poured gasoline into the dens, followed by a lighted match. Edward Hoagland, who spent some time with a coyote hunter when writing his essay "Lament for the Red Wolf," says that "compared to trapping, den-hunting is downright purist and arcane. It's catching the animals alive, by hand, in their hidden home, and some predator hunters hardly bother to trap at all, killing a presentable quota of coyotes just by finding and digging up the year's new dens." Hoagland's hunter knew enough about coyote mentality to know how to find the den: he would let the adult coyote spot him, so that "he will have the benefit of its last quick anxious glance in the direction of the den to guide him on," before he shot it.

The so-called Humane Coyote-Getter, or cyanide gun, was approved for government use in 1939. Also called a go-getter, it consisted of a 15-centimetre (6-inch) hollow aluminum tube that was driven into the ground; a spring mechanism was affixed to the top end, which

Many coyotes are killed each year for their thick pellage, which is mixed with wolf pelts for coats and parka trim. The slump in fur prices has inspired many trappers to call for a re-introduction of the bounty system. JOHN HENDRICKSON held a .38 calibre revolver case loaded with a small amount of gunpowder and sodium cyanide. Since coyotes cannot resist investigating any strange-smelling object within their range, the go-getter was baited with a tuft of sheep's wool smeared with an exotically scented lure—Frank Dobie says that the U.S. Fish and Wildlife Service recommended "a compound of rotten meat, especially horse, armadillo or prairie dog; rotten brains; a tincture of beaver castor; and . . . Siberian musk, which comes from between the toes of Siberian deer." When the coyote investigated the scent, pulling up on the wool with its teeth, it triggered the spring mechanism, which fired the gunpowder, which shot the cyanide up into the coyote's mouth and eyes. Death usually followed before the blinded coyote could run the length of a football field. The go-getter was used almost exclusively for many years, until ranchers began to complain that it was also killing their domestic dogs. "Every year there were dog losses," writes Cadieux. "This aroused much enmity for the coyote trapper." The device is still available, however, under the name M-44, and is still used extensively by sheep ranchers.

The predacide of choice in the 1940s was a wartime chemical known as sodium mono-fluoracetate, or Compound 1080, a poison so effective that only half a kilogram (1 pound) of it was enough to kill about 0.5 million kilograms (1 million pounds) of coyote: the normal dosage was 1.6 grams (½ ounce) of 1080 injected into 45.4 kilograms (100 pounds) of bait. "Compound 1080 does not produce a 'pretty' death," notes Cadieux. Working on the nervous system, it seems to speed up the metabolic processes so that the animal ages and dies in six to eight hours. "A 1080-killed coyote will end up lying on its side, all four feet going through very rapid running motions as it finally dies," Cadieux says. Another observer describes "a frenzy of howls and shrieks of pain, vomiting and retching as froth collects on his tightly drawn lips," and Cadieux calls 1080 "the most inhumane poison ever conceived by man."

Perhaps Cadieux had not heard of thallium, a tasteless, odourless metallic chemical that replaced 1080 in the 1960s. Thallium causes a slow, agonizing death, but only in 60 per cent of its victims; the rest just go blind and lose all their hair, and their toenails and teeth drop out.

All use of poison on public lands in the United States was outlawed by the Nixon administration in 1972, and the following year the Senate passed the Environmental Protection Act, which provided further solace to the beleaguered coyote. It is still legal to hunt coyotes on private land with traps, guns and dogs, however. In Ontario, legislation is being drawn up that will examine the entire question of coyote hunting—one plan is to limit the season to two weeks of the year, as is now the case with deer and partridge hunting, and to impose a bag limit. But elsewhere in Canada coyotes are fair game. According to Arlen Todd of the Alberta Department of the Environment, during the 1980s, when coyote pelts fetched sixty to one hundred dollars in the fur industry, about forty thousand coyotes were killed each year in that province. Today, with the collapse of the fur market, accurate figures are hard to come by, since fewer hunters are registering their kills. Similarly, in Ontario, Mike Buss of the Ministry of Natural Resources says that nearly forty thousand coyotes have been registered by hunters and trappers in the province over the past ten years, but he won't even hazard a guess as to how many actual coyote deaths that figure represents. Trappers have to register their kills only if they plan to sell the pelts, and with pelt prices so low in recent years, most don't bother.

Finally, a word should be said about inadvertent coyote hunting, which in some areas accounts for more coyote deaths than the intentional eradication programs undertaken by farmers. In Banff National Park, for example, according to park biologist Mike Gibeau, more coyotes are killed by automobiles and trains than by natural causes. Out of the eleven radio-collared coyotes in his two-year study of coyote-human interaction in the park, seven were killed by motorists. He calls the twinned highway between Canmore and the Banff townsite Death Valley for coyotes and is opposed to the park's plan to extend the double highway to Lake Louise. Coyotes hunting ground squirrels in the tall grass between the highway's fences are regularly picked off by cars. Distemper and canine parvo, brought into the park by tourists' domestic dogs, are also responsible for a significant rise in coyote pup mortality. "I figure up to 90 per cent of all the coyote deaths in the park are directly caused by humans," says Gibeau. "This is the opposite of what you'd expect a park to be. Normally," he says, "you'd expect a park to be dispersing animals out to an area where there is hunting. But we're not dispersing anything. Instead, we're a black hole; animals come here and are killed."

Despite more than a century of human predation, however, the coyote not only has expanded its range geographically but has also increased its numbers exponentially. As a result, there are more coyotes living in more places than ever before. Adolph Murie's classic study, *Ecology of the Coyote in Yellowstone*, published in 1940, tells a typical story. From 1907 to 1935, when coyote hunting was banned in the park, a total of 4,352 coyotes were trapped and killed, and yet Murie estimated that in 1935 there were more coyotes in the park than there had been at the turn of the century. Most scientists estimate that as many as 75 per cent of all coyotes in a population can be killed annually without causing an overall decline in numbers. It's like the old stories of the Trickster: the more Coyote is persecuted and even killed, the more he comes back in different and more elusive forms.

Coyotes have adapted well to human incursion. Caught stealing a free meal, this one displays submissive behaviour to its curious domestic cousin. MICHAEL H. FRANCIS

Highways are one of the coyote's chief enemies. In Banff National Park, Alberta, more coyotes are killed by cars than die from natural causes. JOHN W. WARDEN

STOCK ANSWERS

Why have coyotes been so determinedly hunted? The simple answers—because they kill domestic livestock and because they kill game animals such as deer and antelope—do not stand up to even the cursory scrutiny they are sometimes given. There are, as described in Part 3, more effective and less costly ways to protect farm animals from predation than by trying to turn the entire continent into a sterilized breeding compound for herbivores.

Coyotes have inherited the reputation of the timber wolf, to a large extent. By an unfortunate accident of history, North America was colonized in the sixteenth century, when the fear of wolves was at its peak in Europe. Europeans brought to North America an attitude towards wolves that is pretty much summed up in such folk tales as "Peter and the Wolf" and "Little Red Riding Hood," stories in which wolves are cunning and malicious stalkers of innocent lambs and children. The behaviour of the velociraptors, about which scientists know almost nothing, in Steven Speilberg's *Jurassic Park* is extrapolated from the imagined ferocity of wolves as depicted in such works of fiction as Jack London's (and now Walt Disney's) *White Fang*. There is a superficial resemblance between the European tales of werewolves, for example—human beings that turn into wolves and kill other human beings—and Native American tales of "skinwalkers," human beings who turn themselves into coyotes and wreak havoc on their enemies. But the differences are instructive: a werewolf is a satanic creature; a skinwalker is a holy man, a man who turns himself into a god.

Barry Lopez, in *Of Wolves and Men*, attributes this hatred of wolves and coyotes to what he calls theriophobia, or "fear of the beast as an irrational, violent, insatiable creature. Fear of the projected beast in oneself." This is a much more generalized fear than the fear of wolves, because it extends to all wild creatures—to all of nature itself. In the five centuries since Columbus, we have systematically tried to wipe out every species that has interfered with what we consider to be our God-given right to exercise dominion over wild as well as domestic animals, over beasts of the forest as well as beasts of the field. In 1931, for example, the U.S. Senate passed legislation calling for "the destruction of all mountain lions, wolves, coyotes, bobcats, prairie dogs, gophers, ground squirrels, jackrabbits and other animals injurious to agriculture, horticulture, forestry, husbandry, game or domestic animals, or that carried disease." The Senate envisioned a North America inhabited by no other animal but livestock and game, nothing but what was controlled by or useful to human beings. Such legislation goes far beyond anything that can be called agricultural management or even predator control. It belongs to the category of revenge.

Coyotes have been chased on snowmobiles and in airplanes and helicopters until they drop dead from exhaustion or heart failure. Their carcasses have been hung on fences as "a warning to other coyotes." Rattlesnakes have been dropped into dens full of pups. In *The*

Carson Factor, an account of a disastrous coyote eradication program in Klamath County, Oregon, in the 1930s, William Ashworth writes:

Otherwise decent men, men fond of their wives and children and tenderly solicitous toward dogs, horses and sheep, have been known to gleefully wire captured coyotes' mouths shut and turn them loose to starve, or to saw off their lower jaws with hacksaws, or to bind gunnysacks around them, douse it with kerosene, and set it afire, or to purposely leave them in traps for up to a week after they have been captured, waiting for their wounds to putrefy and their bodies to dehydrate, making sure that they suffer before they die.

Hope Ryden, describing the public outcry that finally was heard when some of the more inventive methods employed by federal coyote hunters came to light, quotes a letter from Dr. Raymond F. Bock of the Pima Medical Society in Arizona to the U.S. Department of the Interior: "One wonders," wrote Dr. Bock, "whether someone in your department has gone mad from a personal hatred of predators. . . . We wonder what kind of misfits may be perpetrating this campaign."

But the ultimate revenge may still be the Trickster's. Jeremy Schmidt, who lives in Jackson, Wyoming, tells a story about a local rancher who caught a coyote that he suspected had been killing his sheep. Rather than kill the coyote outright, the rancher tied a stick of dynamite to it, lit the dynamite and let the coyote go.

Coyote ran straight under the rancher's brand new pickup truck and lay down.

FACING PAGE: *A coyote carcass hung on a farmer's fence in Oregon. In 1992 alone, Animal Damage Control agents killed 97,966 coyotes in the United States.* THOMAS KITCHIN

Despite attempts at eradication, the coyote has extended its range from such areas as the Mojave Desert, shown here, into most of North America. JEFF FOOTT

PAGE 100: *Coyotes now exist in such disparate places as Alaska, New England and Montana, where these two coyotes were photographed.* ALAN & SANDY CAREY

PART 3

COYOTES & COMMON SENSE

COYOTES & COMMON SENSE

*Through all these new, imaginative, and creative
approaches to the problem of sharing our earth
with other creatures there runs a constant
theme, the awareness that we are dealing with life. . . .*

—Rachel Carson, *Silent Spring*, 1962

CAUGHT IN THE CROSSFIRE

Ontario's Bruce Peninsula is a rocky point of second-growth forest and hard-won farmland
that juts out into Lake Huron to form the western shore of Georgian Bay. It comprises the
province's two main sheep-producing counties and in recent years has been the focus of a
fierce battle over predator control—read coyote hunting. Hunting coyotes here is a traditional winter sport. Sheep farmers with nothing much else to do from November to May
park their pickups along concession and side roads and pick off coyotes with their .303s,
often without even getting out of their cabs. Some of them are paid by the municipality to
do it; others just do it for fun. Coyotes, they all say, are killing sheep, and the only way to
prevent famine in the land is to kill coyotes. The sheep industry in Ontario, like everywhere
else on the continent, is not a healthy one, and coyotes, many sheep farmers believe, are to
blame for it.

Coyote predation on sheep has become a kind of rural myth. In Grey and Bruce counties, about 250 sheep, or 1 per cent of the 25,000 sheep raised on the peninsula, are report-

PAGES 102-103: *A coyote pounces
on a vole.* TOM & PAT LEESON

FACING PAGE: *Coyotes are one of
the few natural enemies of porcu-
pines, although as the quill in the
nose of this coyote in Banff
National Park attests, voles are
much safer prey.* THOMAS
KITCHIN

FACING PAGE: *There is no
denying that some coyotes prey on
livestock, such as sheep, calves and
chickens. In the 1920s, many
western farmers were run out of
business by their inability to
control coyote predation.*
THOMAS KITCHIN

PAGES 108–109: *A coyote howls
near Sheep River, Alberta. Studies
of coyote eating habits in that
province show that sheep make up
less than 3 per cent of coyotes' diet.*
TIM FITZHARRIS

edly killed by coyotes every year. And yet everyone has stories about someone else's livestock being decimated by coyotes. "I've only lost two or three sheep myself," one Bruce County farmer told me, "but a farmer down the road says he loses 50 or 60 lambs a year to coyotes." A Grey County beef and dairy farmer recently told a reporter: "They kill everything in their path when they go through a place. One fella had five coyotes in with his sheep by the barn one morning. Another had a coyote behind the bushes waiting for a calf to be born."

These stories are told about coyotes to justify the reinstatement of the bounty system, whereby the province would pay hunters for every "scalp"—both ears joined by an integument of skin—brought in to the municipal office. The Ontario government officially frowns on bounties now, preferring to compensate farmers for lost livestock rather than pay them to hunt wild animals. In 1989–90, the Ministry of Agriculture and Food paid out $368,000 in compensation for reported coyote- and wolf-killed livestock. The same year, the Ministry of Natural Resources began rigorously enforcing its ban on the bounty system, which had been declared illegal in 1972. Still, taking advantage of a loophole in the legislation, a few municipalities in Grey-Bruce pay hunters from $25 to $50 a day for their trouble. This doesn't exactly provide an incentive to hunters, but it does add a little spice to the sport. Some hunters have taken to importing specially trained dogs from the United States, so-called coyote hounds, cross-bred for speed from the Russian wolfhound and the greyhound. Others place "taste aversion" collars, which are leather pouches laced with a chemical, on their sheep. When a coyote goes for the sheep's throat, it bites into the pouch and ingests the chemical, becoming violently ill and thus averse to killing any more sheep. In Bruce County, I've been told, farmers place Compound 1080 in these collars instead of the aversion chemical: the Department of Agriculture's compensation program pays for the dead sheep, and the municipality's bounty helps to pay for the collars. Buying poison for the purpose of killing coyotes is illegal in Ontario. When I asked an MNR official in Toronto what the penalty would be for anyone caught poisoning a coyote in Ontario, she answered that it is impossible to poison a coyote in Ontario, because buying poison in Ontario is illegal.

The result, in Grey-Bruce as well in hundreds of other agricultural areas in Canada and the United States, has been a steady war on coyotes and a series of confrontations with wildlife biologists, animal rights activists and outraged citizens on one side, and farmers and people who just like to hunt on the other. So far, the biologists and outraged citizens are winning battles, but the war rages on. Allen Smith, president of the Bruce Federation of Agriculture, which favours the reinstatement of the bounty system, has put it succinctly: "There are too many people pushing the animal rights department, influencing MNR decisions," he says. "They want to keep wild animals around."

As usual, Coyote is somewhere in the middle, caught in the crossfire, laughing.

COYOTES AND SHEEP

In the Trickster stories, Coyote is often and even easily killed. In one, he is shot with a magic arrow by Chickadee, who also kills Elk with a flint knife and three wolves by tossing them elk meat wrapped around red-hot rocks. But Coyote, and only Coyote, keeps coming back to life. Elk does not recover from predation, and neither does Wolf. This is as true in nature as it is in mythology. As Donald Worster notes in *Nature's Economy,* "ancient Indian myth says 'brother coyote' will be the last animal alive on earth, and in fact he has already outlasted many of his primeval associates."

The more coyotes that are killed by hunters, trappers and farmers, the more they seem to spring back in even greater numbers. Coyotes are not an endangered or even a threatened species, and hunting them is legal almost anywhere in North America. Although bounties and poison have been outlawed, the coyote is officially defined as a nuisance animal, a furbearer or a game species in most states and provinces: hunting coyotes for sport is as legal and as traditional as hunting deer or ducks, and there are no specified seasons or bag limits for coyotes, as there are for all other game animals. In the state of Kansas, the coyote is one of the few animals that can legally be shot from a vehicle. Even hunting coyotes with specially trained hounds is permitted and is as common in many parts of North America as fox hunting was in England in the nineteenth century. But the coyote is doing just fine, thank you, despite a century and a half of "controls." Perhaps it is time to re-examine our approach to establishing some kind of harmony between coyotes and us.

Except in an extremely localized sense, coyote control does not work; in the long run, leaving coyotes alone might be a more effective way of decreasing their numbers. In Yellowstone, Murie found that after coyote control was halted in 1935, the coyote population density declined naturally, and thus, by 1942, there were fewer coyotes in the park than when controls had been in place. The natural mortality rate for coyotes older than one year of age is from 35 to 40 per cent; when mortality rises, as it does when coyotes are subjected to predator-control programs, the coyote responds by increasing its litter size, raising the percentage of females that become sexually active in their first year and allowing beta females to breed. The result is more coyotes. Conversely, when left to their own devices, coyotes succumb to natural controls—starvation, disease, injuries such as infection from porcupine quills and predation by such animals as mountain lions, rattlesnakes, eagles, grizzlies and wolves. Even elk, normally a prey species, can be predacious when the opportunity arises. In Banff, Mike Gibeau named one of his radio-collared coyotes Lucky, because just as Mike came upon him while checking his trap site, he found a full-grown female elk about to kick the coyote's skull in. "If I hadn't come along when I did," says Mike, "that coyote would have been killed for sure." If all we wanted was fewer coyotes, not hunting them might be the best way to achieve that result. The outcome of all these more or less natural controls is a stable population.

The rationale for human intervention in coyote control is based on a misconception about the nature of coyotes. There is no denying that some coyotes kill old, sick and isolated sheep or cattle, lambs or calves, and a few healthy adults as well. As long ago as the 1930s, biologist Charles C. Sperry examined the stomach contents of 15,000 coyotes collected over a five-year period: his report showed that rabbits made up 33 per cent of the coyote's total diet; carrion was second at 25 per cent; rodents were about 18 per cent; and domestic livestock 13.5 per cent. Even at that, *The Cain Report on Predator Control* in 1970 estimated that the value of sheep and lambs lost to all predators in the twelve western states was $22.3 million, most of which was chalked up to coyotes. In 1978, the U.S. Fish and Wildlife Service calculated that coyote predation alone cost North American sheep farmers $19 million. The latest figures from the U.S. Department of Agriculture state that 500,000 sheep are lost to predation each year, 60 per cent of them to coyotes.

But there is also no doubt that coyotes do much less damage to livestock than is claimed by livestock owners. The Department of Agriculture gets its data from sheep ranchers and, as Donald Schueler pointed out in a profile of the ADC in a recent issue of *Sierra* magazine, such figures "are likely to be highly inflated." Many other animals besides coyotes prey on livestock; in fact, many other canines, including coyote-dog hybrids (coydogs), wolves, wild dogs and domestic dogs, kill livestock. But coyotes generally take the rap: investigations carried out in southwestern Ontario in 1992 found that about half of the 152 livestock attacks reported to the MNR as coyote kills the previous winter were probably the work of coydogs, and another 53 were carried out by domestic dogs running loose. Similar figures are reported wherever livestock compensation programs require official identification of the predating species: what farmers call coyote kills are quite often the work of other predators.

The reason for such misidentification may be that domestic dogs, coydogs and coyotes are practically indistinguishable from a distance. Biologists often have to resort to morphological evidence to define the difference between domestic dog and coyote skulls: they check the narrowness of the animal's snout and measure the ratio of the length of the upper tooth row (first premolar to last premolar) to the palatal width (the distance between the upper first molars). Animals with a ratio of more than 3:1 are usually coyotes; those with ratios of less than 2:7 are dogs. In some of their colour phases, coyotes even resemble wolves: the eastern coyote in Ontario, for example, is almost the same size and colour as the Algonquin wolf, largely because hybridization has caused them to share a lot of the same DNA. Pelts of both species are often thrown in together at fur auctions, making exact records of trapping figures difficult to maintain.

There may also be a more economic explanation: compensation for lost livestock is paid

A coydog, foreground, is a cross between a coyote and a domestic dog. Coyotes are often blamed for damage caused by these hybrid look-alikes. LEONARD LEE RUE III

to farmers out of municipal budgets if a domestic dog does the killing and out of provincial funds if the culprit is a wild animal such as a coyote. Since the inspection of claims is carried out by municipal appointees, there could be a built-in bias towards wild-animal predation as the cause.

Nearly every investigation of reported high coyote predation on farm animals has exonerated the coyote. In British Columbia's Fraser Valley, where in the 1980s local farmers had complained that coyotes were killing their sheep in unconscionable numbers, a two-year study of coyote scat and stomach contents determined that small rodents constituted 70.2 per cent of coyotes' diet and rabbits 8.2 per cent. Most of the rest was made up of raccoon, opossum, muskrat, deer, plants and insects: only 0.2 per cent of coyotes' total diet was sheep, and that could easily be accounted for as carrion.

Sheep production in North America has more than halved in the past three decades as a result of various economic factors—rising production costs, the introduction of synthetic fibres to replace wool, the importation of cheaper meat from New Zealand, as well as increased predation by wild animals—but there is no solid basis for placing a significant amount of the blame on coyotes. Researchers unanimously agree with Marc Bekoff's 1979 study, in which he found little evidence that coyote predation was the primary factor in decreased sheep production: "Coyotes do kill sheep, as well as other livestock and poultry," Bekoff reported in *Scientific American*, adding that "many factors other than coyote predation can cause considerably heavier damage." Bekoff cites a study conducted in the early 1970s that showed that in Idaho, where $2.3 million in sheep losses had been reported in one year, 36 per cent was attributed to disease, 30 per cent to "unspecified causes" and 34 percent to predation: only 14.3 per cent of those losses could be traced to coyotes. Most sheep farmers curse disease, the high cost of feed and disobliging weather as much as they rail against predating coyotes, but, as one Bruce County farmer puts it, "coyotes are the only one we can do much about."

Even if coyotes were primarily responsible for the sheep farmers' woes, killing them is not an effective means of protecting flocks. In fact, it may have exactly the opposite effect—not only because coyote numbers tend to increase when the population is exploited but also because of the kind of coyotes that survive the control measures. Bob Crabtree argues that killing adult coyotes at certain times of the year could actually result in an increase in lamb predation. "When the pups are a few weeks old, in early to mid-May," he says, "they place enormous pressure on the adults in the pack to provide them with food, and that's when the adults just go out and get the fastest protein source they can find. In some areas, that will be spring lambs rather than mice. Now, what happens if you kill off some of those adults? You end up with fewer adults having to provide the same number of pups with fast meat. What will they do? They'll go out and kill more lambs."

grams (15,000 pounds) of carrion was normally exposed in this way each winter. In 1973, Todd convinced farmers in two other townships to burn small carcasses (poultry and piglets) and to use dead-stock removal companies for larger carcasses, thus reducing the amount of carrion available to coyotes to about 680 kilograms (1,500 pounds). There was some initial opposition to Todd's experiment; farmers thought that without carrion either the coyotes would leave the area, causing an increase in rodents that would lead to an increase in crop damage, or else packs of "hunger-driven" coyotes would simply turn from feeding on dead stock to preying on livestock. Which of the two possibilities would actually happen was exactly what Todd wanted to find out.

He found that in areas where carrion was unavailable, the coyotes either increased their consumption of rodents or else moved to another area—usually the area in which carrion was still being left out. In December and January, both carrion-free townships showed a 93 per cent decline in coyote population, with a consequent decrease in livestock predation. Perhaps more significantly, there was no increase in livestock depredation in the two control townships, even though many of the coyotes leaving the experimental area went to the control area in search of carrion.

A coyote hunts voles on a frosty morning. Studies show that coyotes prefer low, rodent-rich valleys to high meadows, where bighorn sheep are plentiful. TOM & PAT LEESON

ABOVE: *Coyotes catch small prey
like pocket gophers every 20
minutes.* MICHAEL S. QUINTON

FACING PAGE: *Coyotes
successfully run down rodents
about 60 per cent of the time.*
W. PERRY CONWAY

Two coyotes pull down a white-tailed deer in mid-ford. Being smaller than wolves, coyotes use running water or deep snow to aid them in hunting. MICHAEL H. FRANCIS

COYOTES AND DEER

Defending domestic livestock herds is not the only reason given for the war against coyotes. More than a few hunters admit that their aim is also to protect deer or other game populations from overpredation—the more coyotes they kill, in other words, the more deer will be available for them to kill as well.

This attitude is a holdover from earlier times. Adolph Murie noted in 1940 that predator control in the park began only "when hunting was so wanton as to imperil the existence of game animals," the object of coyote control being to eliminate "any factor which might be considered in any way inimical to the well-being of the game"—any factor, that is, except game hunting itself. There was absolutely no scientific support for the supposition that coyotes were depleting deer or elk populations in the park (or anywhere else). But from 1877 on, a fierce battle against all predators was waged in Yellowstone, and strychnine-laced carcasses led to the eradication of wolves, wolverines and mountain lions by the mid-1920s. Murie quotes the 1889 report by park superintendent F. A. Boutelle, which stated that "the carnivora of the park have, in common with other animals, increased until, I believe, something should be done for their extermination." As Murie notes sourly, the fact that game animals were increasing did not seem to incline park authorities to a reconsideration of their attitude towards predators. "In Superintendant Anderson's report for 1896," he writes, "coyote control is recommended because the animals were numerous, not because they were injurious."

The report by Superintendant George Woods for 1909 veers breathtakingly close to sentience: "Quite a number of coyotes were killed last year," Woods wrote, "about 60—but still they seem to increase. It is doubtful, however, if they kill much game, as the deer seem able to protect themselves. On several occasions last winter, I saw deer chasing coyotes instead of being chased by them." But still the war went on: in 1910, a total of 40 coyotes were killed in the park; in 1911, the total was 129; in 1912, it was 240. From 1907 to 1935, a grand total of 4,352 coyotes was expunged from the park, along with 132 grey wolves (the last one was killed in 1925) and 121 mountain lions.

Murie's study showed that Woods's speculation that coyotes do not feed much on deer was quite correct. From an analysis of coyote scat samples over several years, Murie determined that deer and elk constitued only 17.1 per cent of the coyotes' total diet, the bulk being composed of field mice (33.9 per cent) and pocket gophers (21.6 per cent). Snowshoe hares comprised 3.4 per cent, and grasshoppers 7.9 per cent. He also found that most of the deer and elk ingested by coyotes was in the form of carrion—animals that had died naturally of age or disease or starvation, not of coyote predation.

More recent studies have borne Murie's observations out. In Alberta, Arlen Todd studied the stomach contents of 542 coyotes trapped in the forested regions of that province between 1972 and 1975 and found that ungulates provided only 11 per cent of the coyotes' total diet. In contrast, up to 77 per cent consisted of snowshoe hare. In fact, Todd found that coyote populations fluctuated according to the abundance of hares, not ungulates. Murie had anticipated these findings in 1942, when in a study of wolves in Mount McKinley National Park he noticed that coyotes did not inhabit the upper ranges, where mountain sheep were plentiful, but preferred to remain in the lower valleys where "the staple rodent supply is more abundant."

Although some studies show that in parts of New England the eastern coyote may have a significant impact on white-tailed deer populations—especially in years when the number of deer is high and the number of snowshoe hares is low—the consensus is that ungulate predation by coyotes is not as significant in determining their numbers as are other factors, such as the amount of precipitation during the previous summer. "Throughout most of their range in [Ontario]," write the authors of the MNR report "Wolves and Coyotes in Ontario," "coyotes have caused relatively little damage either to wildlife or livestock, and on the balance sheet they should be classed as beneficial to the economy." In fact, the report says that "we have no authentic reports of coyotes attacking deer in this province." The report lists field mice as the coyote's principal food source, comprising nearly 30 per cent of its diet, followed by rabbits and hares (15 to 40 per cent), groundhogs (in summer, until the end of August) and just about anything else that is edible, "either vegetable or animal . . . , " including apples and even wheat.

Even in areas where coyotes are killing deer, killing coyotes may have no effect on the number of predations on deer. The Maine Department of Inland Fisheries and Wildlife (MDIFW) has recently rejected the reintroduction of bounties in that state to control coyote predation of deer, because, it said, "bounties are generally not effective in reducing predation, are subject to fraud, and . . . serve only to subsidize a small number of hunters with no increase in overall numbers of the prey species the bounty is intended to protect." As MDIFW biologist Henry Hilton points out, this is because "the fall coyote trap harvest is predominantly juvenile animals, and . . . the most damage-causing coyotes are dominant adults." In other words, the animals caught by bounty hunters would not be the same animals that were killing deer.

Perhaps the real question ought not to be whether top predators kill ungulates —of course they do—but rather whether ungulate herds are harmed by such predation. Under natural circumstances, over time, they are not. A study conducted in the Welder Wildlfe Refuge in southern Texas, for example, determined that more than 50 per cent of fawn mortality in white-tailed deer was attributable to coyote predation, and yet the deer herds continued to thrive. To test the effects of coyote predation, the researchers fenced off a 391-

hectare (966-acre) "exclosure" and removed the coyotes from within it so that the deer population inside was effectively unbothered by coyotes for five years. What they found is worth quoting in full:

> Deer densities within the exclosure . . . tripled compared to outside, remained stable for two to three years, and then declined precipitously to levels only slightly above those recorded outside the exclosure. Forage for deer within the exclosure deteriorated significantly. The general health of the deer declined noticeably and parasite loads increased. Ultimately, the decrease in early postnatal mortality was compensated by increased mortality among fawns six to twelve months of age. Coyotes clearly were affecting survival of young deer. The removal of fawns by coyotes at earlier ages apparently helped maintain the remaining herd in much better physical condition.

Murie found more or less the same thing in Yellowstone in 1940. He concluded that coyotes exerted a "negligible" effect on the park's elk population; after decades of virtually unchallenged predation, he reported, they had made "no appreciable inroads in the populations of deer, antelope and bighorn sheep." In fact, Murie suggested that deer herds may even be improved *mentally* by coyote predation: coyotes teach them wariness, which protects them from all predators.

Coyote predation on deer herds may actually be less damaging to the population than human hunting, since human hunters tend to take adults in their prime, thus culling the best of the herds rather than the worst, as coyotes and wolves do.

PAGES 126–127: *A coyote in Yellowstone National Park gives chase in winter. The coyote's large paws give it an advantage over elk in all but the deepest, softest snow.*
W. PERRY CONWAY

Whether defending an elk carcass from other coyotes in Yellowstone, above, or driving off marauding ravens in Montana, right, the ears-back, teeth-bared stance says, "Keep off." ABOVE: HENRY H. HOLDSWORTH; RIGHT: ALAN & SANDY CAREY

ABOVE: *Rolling in carrion is a popular canid pastime.* BILL BYRNE

PAGES 130–131: *Mountain sheep are not threatened by coyotes: Adolph Murie "found no evidence of coyote predation on the bighorn" in Yellowstone.* MICHAEL S. QUINTON

THE COYOTE'S ROLE IN NATURE

In the tales of the Shuswap of the Northwest Pacific Coast, Coyote created Klamath County, Oregon. In the beginning there was no land, only a single great lake. Coyote came along in a canoe, looked down into the water and saw Pocket Gopher's lodge, called Pocket Gopher up and asked his help in setting things right. Pocket Gopher opened his mouth and produced fish, roots and berries. Coyote created mountains and gave names to the mountain lion, the bear, the elk and the deer. Then he created smoke, a sure sign that he had also created people, and "the people increased rapidly, and the animals and plants on the mountains multiplied."

In the early 1940s, the citizens of Klamath County, Oregon, instituted an intensive campaign to eradicate the coyote from their farmlands. Over a period of a few years, and by a variety of methods, more than ten thousand coyotes were killed. By 1947, there was not a single coyote in Klamath County. But there were field mice: in the absence of any natural control, the rodent population exploded. In 1947, the field mouse population alone was estimated at 25,000 per hectare (10,000 per acre); the cost in lost crops soared into the millions of dollars, far more than had ever been attributed to damage by coyotes. The cost of exterminating the field mice was also high; the incident is known to history as the Mouse War. In the end, Klamath County began to reintroduce the coyote to its farmlands. The whole exercise, from coyote extirpation to mouse eradication to coyote reintroduction, was an object lesson in understanding the balance of nature before blundering in to tamper with it.

We still do not understand the role of every animal in the ecosystem. As Mike Gibeau puts it, "Nature is like a balloon; we know that if we squeeze one end of it, it's going to bulge out somewhere else. We just never know where." And yet we persist in the belief that we can control nature, that in fact nature requires our control to run efficiently and effectively. The coyote, like other predators, has come to be a symbol of this attitude. In *Nature's Economy*, Donald Worster notes that "the coyote has been the object of America's concentrated moralistic fervor, and his tenacious survival represents an outrageous defiance of man's righteous empire over nature."

Worster suggests that "in the twentieth century, the coyote, along with other varmints and predators, has come to be viewed in a radically different light by many Americans." In this new light, a world without predators is seen as "a world that is in trouble." This is true. Klamath County certainly saw it that way after it had gone through the Mouse War. In many areas today, the coyote is not as "cordially detested," as John Muir put it in 1872, "by nearly all cultured people." Pat Wolff, manager of a group of wildlife defenders in Santa Fe, New Mexico, called Forest Guardians, has been working for years to abolish such government-sponsored programs as that carried out by the ADC. "When I first learned about ADC's war on wildlife and saw photos of animals being tortured and killed," she says, "it outraged me that a federal agency should be slaughtering wildlife for the benefit of the ranchers—with taxpayers' money." Elsewhere, biologists and animal-rights defenders are working to educate the public about the beneficial role predators perform in keeping rodent populations down and ungulate herds healthy. We are beginning to appreciate the extent to which tampering with a single strand of nature alters the whole fabric.

But many of us still tend to regard nature as a kind of living museum; if we remove one exhibit, we feel, we will not harm the entire display. This has been reflected in our various national parks policies since the setting aside of Yellowstone and Banff in the 1870s, it has given rise to the idea of "good" animals and "bad" animals, and it is still very much a part of the way we think about nature today—witness the continued wolf eradication programs in Alaska and the Yukon, and the pressure being placed on the Ontario government to eradicate the coyote from Grey and Bruce counties. One of the first repercussions of the recent disclosure by geneticists that the red wolf, an endangered species, may in fact be a cross between wolves and coyotes was a petition from Texan ranchers to remove the red wolf from protection under the Environmental Protection Act because the EPA does not apply to hybrids, even though hybridization is a natural mechanism by which new species are created.

Nature is not a museum, it is an organic system, and the removal of any link in its unfathomable chain weakens the whole and impoverishes us all in ways we cannot know. Coyotes remind us of this simple truth. Our attempts to remove the coyote from our midst are a symbol of our arrogant assumption that we can control nature, bend it to our will, alter it in ways that are beneficial to us. The real consequences of that assumption are apparent today in the devastation we have wrought upon our environment. We need to progress from arrogance to wisdom. Perhaps by studying and appreciating the coyote's role in nature, we will learn much about our own place in it as well.